To My Love

_____

With All My Heart

_____

Letters To My Husband

Letters To My Husband

Letters To My Husband

Letters To My Husband

Letters To My Husband

Letters To My Husband

Letters To My Husband

Letters To My Husband

Letters To My Husband

Letters To My Husband

Letters To My Husband

Letters To My Husband

Letters To My Husband

Letters To My Husband

Letters To My Husband

Letters To My Husband

Letters To My Husband

Letters To My Husband

Letters To My Husband

Letters To My Husband

Letters To My Husband

Letters To My Husband

Letters To My Husband

Letters To My Husband

Letters To My Husband

Letters To My Husband

Letters To My Husband

Letters To My Husband

Letters To My Husband

Letters To My Husband

Letters To My Husband

Letters To My Husband

Letters To My Husband

Letters To My Husband

Letters To My Husband

Letters To My Husband

Letters To My Husband

Letters To My Husband

Letters To My Husband

Letters To My Husband

Letters To My Husband

Letters To My Husband

Letters To My Husband

Letters To My Husband

Letters To My Husband

Letters To My Husband

Letters To My Husband

Letters To My Husband

Letters To My Husband

Letters To My Husband

Letters To My Husband

Letters To My Husband

Letters To My Husband

Letters To My Husband

Letters To My Husband

Letters To My Husband

Letters To My Husband

Letters To My Husband

Letters To My Husband

Letters To My Husband

Letters To My Husband

Letters To My Husband

Letters To My Husband

Letters To My Husband

Letters To My Husband

Letters To My Husband

Letters To My Husband

Letters To My Husband

Letters To My Husband

Letters To My Husband

Letters To My Husband

Letters To My Husband

Letters To My Husband

Letters To My Husband

Letters To My Husband

Letters To My Husband

Letters To My Husband

Letters To My Husband

Letters To My Husband

Letters To My Husband

Letters To My Husband

Letters To My Husband

Letters To My Husband

Letters To My Husband

Letters To My Husband

Letters To My Husband

Letters To My Husband

Letters To My Husband

Letters To My Husband

Letters To My Husband

Letters To My Husband

Letters To My Husband

Letters To My Husband

Letters To My Husband

Letters To My Husband

Letters To My Husband

Letters To My Husband

Letters To My Husband

Letters To My Husband

Letters To My Husband

Letters To My Husband

Letters To My Husband

Letters To My Husband

Letters To My Husband

Letters To My Husband

Letters To My Husband

Letters To My Husband

Letters To My Husband

Letters To My Husband

Letters To My Husband

Letters To My Husband

Letters To My Husband

Letters To My Husband

Letters To My Husband

Letters To My Husband

Letters To My Husband

Letters To My Husband

Letters To My Husband

Letters To My Husband

Letters To My Husband

Letters To My Husband

Letters To My Husband

Letters To My Husband

Letters To My Husband

Letters To My Husband

Letters To My Husband

Made in the USA
Monee, IL
19 March 2022